LOCAL RED BOOK

SITTINGBOUR

FAVERSHAM

LEYSDOWN-ON-SEA · MINSTER · SHEERNESS

C000225336

LEGEND

	~~Substrianized / Restricted Access~~ Restricted Access
	Track
	Built Up Area
- - - - -	Footpath
	Stream
	River
Lock	Canal
━━●━━	Railway / Station
●	Post Office
P P+	Car Park / Park & Ride
C	Public Convenience
+	Place of Worship
→	One-way Street
i	Tourist Information Centre
8 8	Adjoining Pages
	Area Depicting Enlarged Centre
	Emergency Services
	Industrial Buildings
	Leisure Buildings
	Education Buildings
	Hotels etc.
	Retail Buildings
	General Buildings
	Woodland
	Orchard
	Recreation Ground
	Cemetery

CONTENTS

Page Layout & Road Map   **2**
3 Miles to 1 Inch

Street Maps   **3-17**
4 Inches to 1 Mile

Index to Streets   **18**

Red Books showing the way

…eet plans prepared and published by ESTATE PUBLICATIONS, Bridewell House, …NTERDEN, KENT. The Publishers acknowledge the co-operation of the local authorities of …ns represented in this atlas.

Ordnance Survey® This product includes mapping data licensed from Ordnance Survey® with the permission of the Controller of Her Majesty's Stationery Office.

www.ESTATE-PUBLICATIONS.co.uk

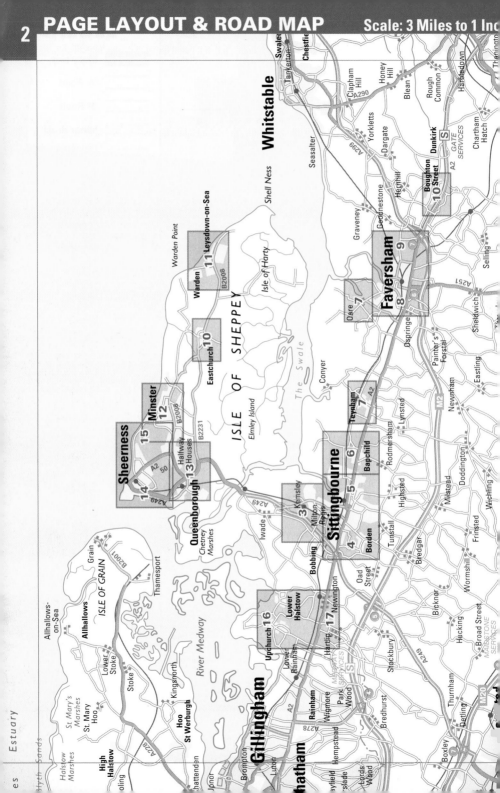

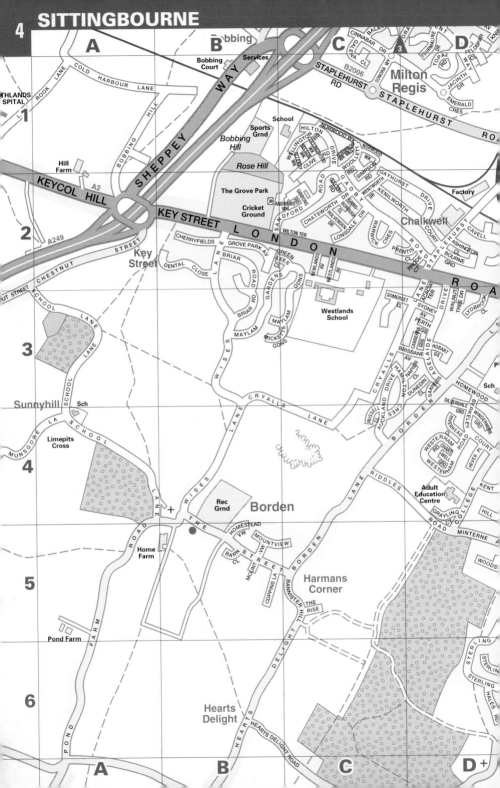

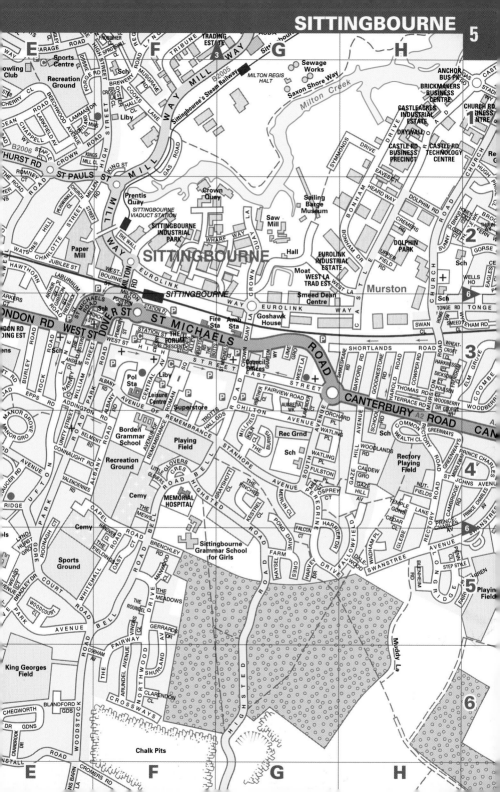

BAPCHILD

6

A · B · C · D

1
Eurolink
ANCHOR BUS PK
MAKERS BUSINESS CENTRE
CASTLE RD TECHNOLOGY CENTRE
CHURCH RD BUSINESS CENTRE
CASTLE WY
GAS
STADIUM
CASTLE ROAD
Sittingbourne Football Club
Mere Court
Recreation Ground
Telegraph Hill
BLACKETTS
ROAD

2
CHURCH ROAD
HUGH PRICE CL
OAK RD
HARRIS GDNS
BURNUP BK
BROOM RD
FIELDER RD
FAIRFIELD
HUTCHINGS
BLYTHE
EAST HALLOWELL LANE
HEARNE
HONEY PK
THISTLE CL
THURN
BRACKEN CL
FERN WK
WALK
GORSE ROAD
BROOM RD
OAK ROAD
PORTLAND AV
CERES CT
EAGLES CL
Sch
WELLS HO
Sch
MEERES CT LA
Oak Rd
East Hall
West Tonge Farm
Club House
The Oast Golf Centre
St Giles Houses
CHURCH ROAD

3
TONGE RD
TONGE ROAD
ALL SAINTS ROAD
FAVERSHAM RD
SMEED
HOME
WHET
HARKNESS CT
DICKSON CT
POULSEN CT
WOODBERRY DR
ELM GROVE
COOMBE DRIVE
LANSDOWN DRIVE
PEEL
WOODBERRY AV
KESWICK
VINCENT RD
AMBLESIDE
GEORGE ST
BEACONSFIELD
GLADSTONE RD
SALISBURY CL
PALMERSTON WK
GORDON
RISEBERRY
DRIVE
LOMAS
ROAD
Snipeshill
Tonge Castle (remains of)
SCRAPS HILL
LOWER LANE
Bunces Farm

4
ROAD
CANTERBURY ROAD FOX HILL THE STREET LONDON
GREENWAYS
PRINCE CHARLES AV
JOHNS AVENUE
CAMBRIDGE RD
PRINCE CHARLES AV
PRINCE
A2
GREENWAYS
AVENUE
SWANSTREE
School
Schs
Sports Centre
Snipeshill
St. Lawrence
Sch
SCHOOL LA
ASHTEAD DR
WINTRED
MORRIS DR
DOUBLE CT
DOUBLEDA
LORDS
AVENT WY
WK
HEMPSTEAD LANE
Bapchild
Hampstead Farm
Cricket Ground

5
VICTORY ROAD
PRINCE CHARLES
PENN
STEP STILE
FAIRLEE WARREN
SWANSTREE
College
Bapchild Court
SCHOOL LANE
ST LAWRENCE
ROAD
SPOONERS DALE
FANTENY
STREET
Morris Court
Haywood
DULLY ROAD
Radfield

6
Playing Field
CHURCH LANE
Rodmersham
Little Dully
RO

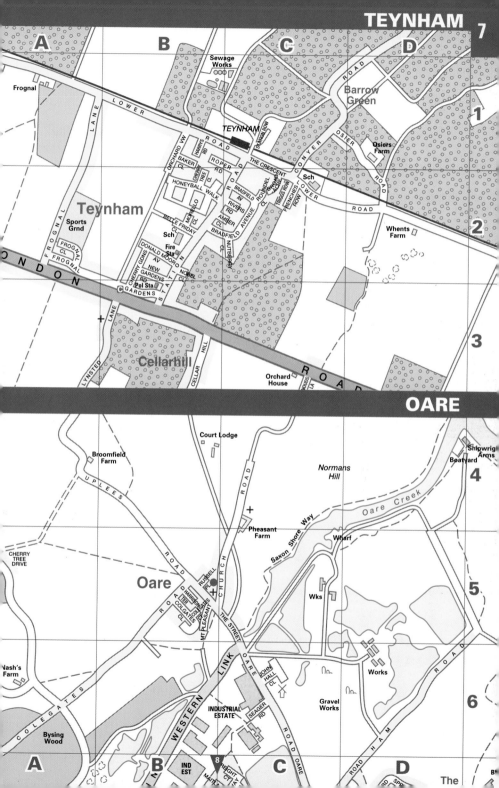

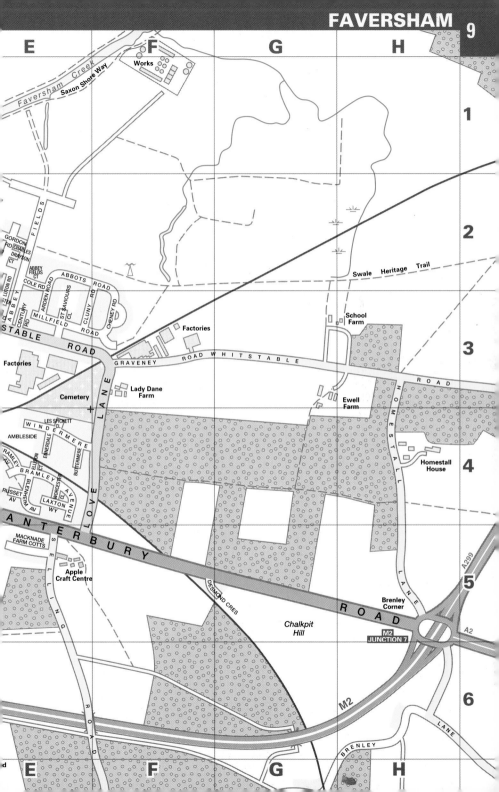

FAVERSHAM

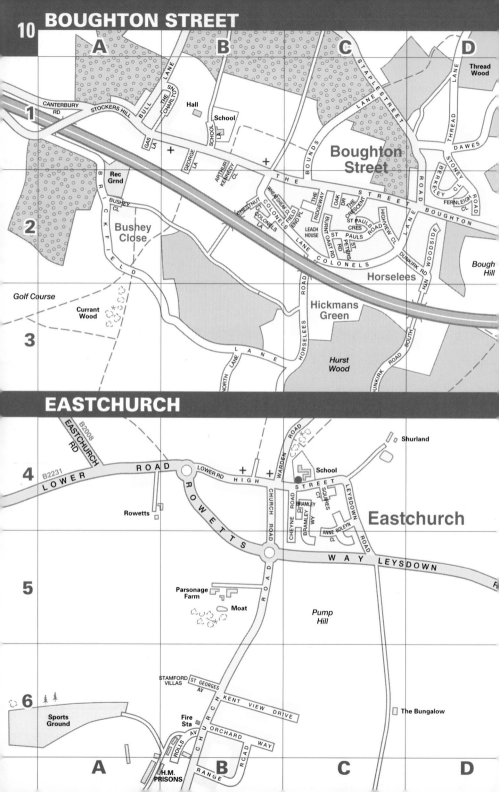

BOUGHTON STREET

A B C D

Thread Wood

CANTERBURY RD
STOCKERS HILL
BULL LANE
THE SN
CHARLTO
Hall
School
SCHOOL LA
GAS LA
GEORGE LA
ARTHUR
KENNEDY CL
+
+
Rec Grnd
BRICKFIELD
BUSHEY CL
Bushey Close
CHESTNUT
WHEATSHEAF CL
COLONELS CT
COLONELS LA
LEACH HOUSE
COLONELS LA
THE RIDGEWAY
FIELD END PL
OAK DR
THE CRESCENT
BURNT OAST RD
ST PAULS CRES
ST PAULS RD
ST PETERS RD
HIGHVIEW CL
PAULS ROAD
DUNKIRK RD
WOODSIDE
THE STREET
BOUNDS
STAPLESTREET LANE
BOUGHTON ROAD
STONEY CL
BERKELEY CL
FERNLEIGH CL
DAWES
THREAD LANE
Boughton Street
Bough Hill
Horselees
HORSELEES ROAD
Golf Course
Currant Wood
Hickmans Green
Hurst Wood
NORTH LANE
LANE
DUNKIRK ROAD SOUTH

1
2
3

EASTCHURCH

EASTCHURCH RD
B2008
B2231
LOWER ROAD
Rowetts
ROWETTS
LOWER RD
HIGH
WARDEN ROAD
+
+
School
Shurland
STREET
CHURCH ROAD
CHEYNE ROAD
BRAMLEY
BRAMLEY WY
SQUIRES
ANNE BOLEYN CL
LEYSDOWN ROAD
Eastchurch
WAY LEYSDOWN
Parsonage Farm
Moat
ROAD
Pump Hill
The Bungalow
Sports Ground
STAMFORD VILLAS
ST GEORGES AV
KENT VIEW DRIVE
ROLLS AV
Fire Sta
CHURCH ROAD
RANGE
ORCHARD WAY
H.M. PRISONS

4
5
6

A B C D

Leysdown
-on-Sea

Warden

Bay View

Thorn Hill

The Bay

Leysdown Coastal Park

Football Ground

Nutts Caravan Site

Camp Site

Bus Depot

Priory Hill Camp

South Bank Holiday Camp

Pol Sta

Harts Holiday Camp

Eastern Holiday Camp

Loves Holiday Camp

Sheppey Holiday Camp

Vanity Farm Holiday Camp

Paradise Gardens

Warden Bay Hotel

Boating Lake

Happy Valley

Cemy

Seaview Holiday Camp

Warden Bay Caravan Park

Warden Bay Holiday Camp

Coronation Chalet Camp

Mustards

B2231

ROAD

SEAVIEW AV

SHURLAND AV

WING

SHELLNESS ROAD

PARK AV

PRIORY CL

PARK AV

NUTTS CT

MANOR WAY

THAMES CT

GROVE AV

EASTERN PROMENADE

THE PROMENADE

SAND CT

LEYSDOWN ROAD

BAY

ROAD

WARDEN

CONDOR CL

CLIFF VW

GDNS

BEACH APPROACH

SEA VIEW GDNS

ST CLEMENTS GDNS

EMERALD GDNS

MELODY LN

CLIFF VW

WATERSIDE

SEASALTER CL

CLIFF CL

IMPERIAL DRIVE

ST JAMES

APPROACH

CLARENCE GDNS

LEICESTER RD

CLIFF DRIVE

PRESTON HALL GDNS

HILSEA

EMPRESS GDNS

WINDSOR GDNS

KNOLL WAY

BUCKLERS

ROAD

CORONATION DR

ST CLEMENTS RD

BAY VIEW GARDENS

CLIFF VW GDNS

OCEAN DR

MUSTARDS

DANES DR

DANES DRIVE

WARDEN VIEW GARDENS

JETTY

CLIFF

ROAD

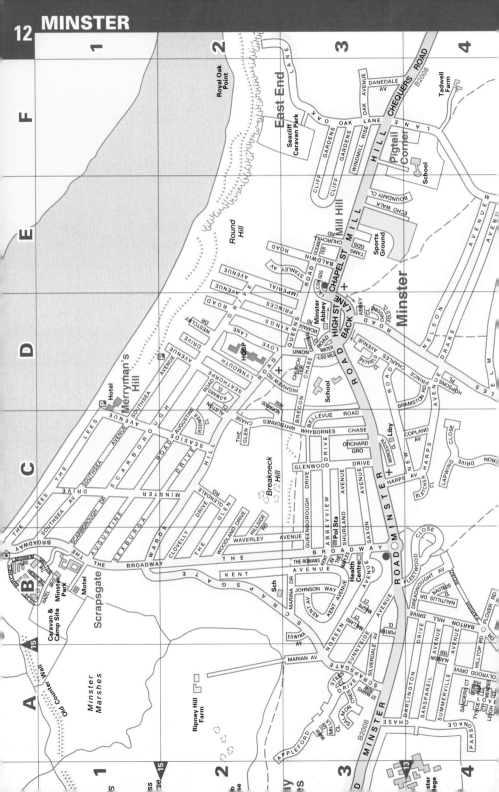

Minster

East End

Minster Marshes

Scrapsgate

Merryman's Hill

Round Hill

Breakneck Hill

Royal Oak Point

Ripney Hill Farm

Tadwell Farm

Pigtail Corner

Seacliff Caravan Park

Sports Ground

Minster Abbey

Minster Park

Caravan & Camp Site

Old Corner Wall

CHEQUERS ROAD

MINSTER ROAD

THE BROADWAY

SOUTHSEA AVENUE

SCARBOROUGH DRIVE

AUGUSTINE ROAD

SEXBURGA DRIVE

CLOVELLY DRIVE

WOODLAND DRIVE

GLENDALE RD

WARDS RD

THE GLEN

SEASIDE AVENUE

LEES

THE LEES

LYNMOUTH

SEATHORPE AVE

ALSTON RD

HOWARD AVE

ST AUGUSTINE RD

HILL

LOVE LANE

NORMAN RISE

WHYBORNES CHASE

GLENWOOD DRIVE

QUEENBOROUGH DRIVE

WAVERLEY AVENUE

HILLSIDE RD

KENT AVENUE

BELLEVUE ROAD

WHYBORNES CHASE

ORCHARD GRO

ABBEYVIEW DRIVE

SHURLAND AVENUE

SAXON AVENUE

THE MAPLES

THE ROWANS

MARINA DR

JOHNSON WAY

KENT AVENUE

EDWINA AV

MARIAN AV

NOREEN AV

SUNNYSIDE AV

SILVERDALE AV

SCRAPSGATE

MALLARD CT

MAGPIE CT

PORTER CL

DREADNOUGHT AV

NAUTILUS DR

HILL DRIVE

BARTON DRIVE

HILLTOP RD

PLOVER RD

PARISH

ALADDIN TER

ALYWOOD DRIVE

TYSOE CT

SANDERS CT

SUMMERVILLE AVE

SANSPAREIL AVE

DARLINGTON DRIVE

FLEETWOOD AV

CLOSE

COPLAND AV

HARPS AV

NEW HARPS

LAPWING DRIVE

DRIVE

CLOSE

NELSON ROAD

DRAKE AVENUE

AVENUE

CHARLES ROAD

PRINCE AVENUE

PETFIELD RD

BRAMSTON ROAD

HOPSONS RD

WORCESTER CL

Liby

Health Centre

Pol Sta

Sch

Motel

Hotel

HOSP

School

School

Minster College

CLIFF GARDENS

CLIFF GARDENS

OAK LANE

OAK AVENUE

DANEDALE AV

WINDMILL RISE

MILL HILL

ECHO WALK

BOUNDARY CL

CHAPEL ST

HIGH ST

BACK LANE

CHURCH RD

CHURCH ST

STANLEY AV

IMPERIAL AVENUE

PRINCES AVENUE

KINGS AVENUE

QUEENS AVENUE

UNION ROAD

BALDWIN RD

TAMS GDS

WATER LOO HILL

VICARAGE RD

HIGHVIEW RD

BRECON CHASE

THIRD AVENUE

THE BROADWAY

KENT AVENUE

THE GATE

THE GLEN

SALMON CRES

MILLS AV

APPLEFORD

ROAD

B2008

B2008

15

15

15

13

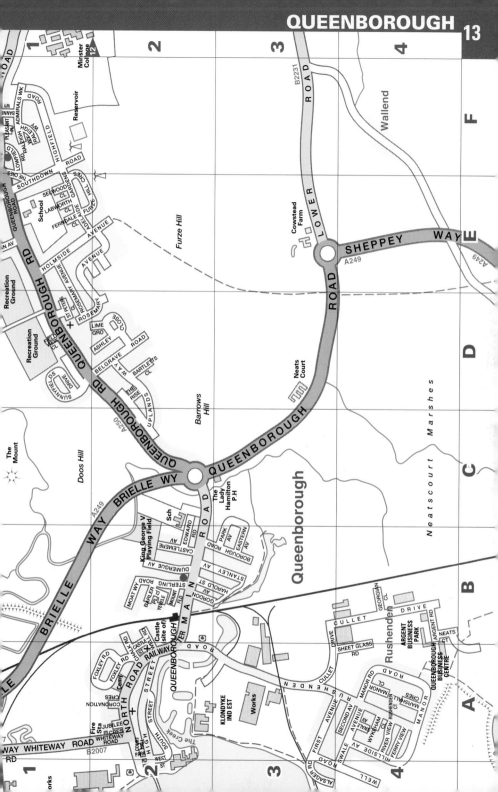

E F G H

1

2

THAMES ESTUARY

Cheyney Rock

Bartons Point

Monument

CRESPLANADE
MARINE PARADE
PALMAR
STREET
ST JAMES ST
CLYDE ST
UNITY ST
ROAD
ROAD
RICHMOND
NURSERY CL
JEFFERSON ROAD
BARNSLEY CR
SEAGER ROAD
BECKLEY RD

Marine Town

Schools

Playing Field

Ship on Shore P.H.

Barton's Point
Coastal Park

Old Counter Wall

Boating Lake

SILVER BIRCHES
HAZEL GRO
FIR GREEN
THE WILLOWS
VIBURNUM

Caravan &
Camp Site

Minster
Park

Scrapsgate

Motel

THE SOU
SCARBOR
JGUSTI
SEXBURG

3

4

Sheerness
Holiday
Village

MINSTER MARSHES

Minster
Marshes

THE BROADWAY

WARDS
CLOVELLY
WOODLAND
WAVERLEY
HILLS
AVENUE
QUEENBO

12

5

Sheerness
Golf Course

Driving
Range

Ripney Hill
Farm

POWER STATION ROAD

Works

Club
House

ST KATHERINE RD
WILLIAM DR
BUDDLE RD
RIGBY DR
SCOTCHMEN CL

FILER RD

DANLEY RD

Halfway
Houses

APPLEFORD

MARIAN AV

SCRAPSGATE
KENT
THE AV

EDWINA
MARINA DR
KENT AV
JOHNSON CT
KENT AVENUE

Sch

THE REMARKS
THE MAPLES

ABBE
Pol St
SHURLA

6

Cemetery

School

EASTERN AV
WESTERN AV
HILDA ROAD
LYNSTED RD
BELMONT RD

QUEENBOROUGH
ROAD

MINSTER
THE CRES
LOWFIELD
PLEASANT PL
LEIGH
BANNER
ADMIRALS WK
WY

B2008

ROAD

MINSTER

B2008

MARIN
MILLS
CL
SALMON CRES
APPLEFORD

STILES
NOREEN
SUNNYSIDE
SILVERDALE AV

MIDLAND CT
MAPLE
AVENUE
PORT
Health
Centre
SAXON

QUEENBO
ROAD

School

Recreation
Ground

SCHOOL

13

SAXON

BROAD

H

F

G

Great Barksore Farm

Lower Halstow

Elm Farm

WARDWELL LANE

School

Broom Downs

Halstow Creek

Wharf

VICARAGE LANE

CHURCH PATH

CROUCH HILL

SHEERNESS

WESTMORLAND CT

CUMBERLAND DR

BURNTWICK DR

SCHOOL LA

SCHOOL RD

Twinney Wharf

Sewage Works

HERON CL

CURLEW

WING DR

THE GREEN

LANDRAIL RD

BELL CROWN RD

LA

THE

LANE

Westfield Cottages

The Laurels

WESTFIELD COTTAGES

Boxted

BOXTED LANE

Frog Farm

Holywell Farm

SUSANS LANE

Cricket Ground

HOLYWELL LANE

HOLYWELL LANE

BEACH

HOLYWELL LANE

POOT LANE

Wetham Green

THE POLES

STREET

Upchurch

FORGE LANE

WALSTOW LANE

CHURCH FARM RD

Sch

THE POLES

Hall

CRESSET CT

HORSHAM

HORSHAM HILL

Horsham Farm

Horsham Marsh

BRADSHAW

Post Office

Rec Grnd

BISHOP LA

DRAKES CLOSE

CHAFFES CLOSE

MARSTAN CL

CHAFFES

WALLBRIDGE LANE

Golf Course

Gore Farm

GORE COTTAGES

Club House

CANTERBURY LANE

Wardwell Wood

Keycol Hill

Boyse's Hill Farm

Keyco

Cranbrook Wood

NEWINGTON ENTERPRISE CENTRE

St Mary's Church

Church Farm

St Martins Cl

St Stephens Pl

St Marks Pl

St Matthews Cl

Edwins Pl

Newington

ELLENS PL

BOYCES HILL

STREET

Cemy

Sch

VICARAGE CT

DENHAM RD

WESTWOOD WK

HASTED CL

NEWINGTON CL

PRIMROSE CL

DAFFODIL CT

STATION RD

WICKHAM CL

HIGH

CHURCH

CALLAWAYS

RED ROBIN

TRACIES

THE LILAC

BROOKES PL

SCOTTS

Newington Manor

THE WILLOWS

ROAD

LANE

Denhole (site of)

ROMAN

ROAD

Mill Hill

NORTON

CLOSE

FRIENDS

PLAYSTOOL

FRANK APPS

PLAYSTOOL

CL

PEAR TREE WALK

ALLSWORTH

PLAYSTOOL DRIVE

BRAMLEY CL

PEAR TREE WK

ORCHARD

Pond Farm

Rec Grnd

Standard Hill

Denhole

Breach

Breach Farm

NEWINGTON INDUSTRIAL ESTATE

Paradise Farm

Lower Hartlip

HARTLIP

BOXTED

SCHOOL LANE

LONDON

Gore House

LANE

A2

Culvers Hill

Hartlip Hill

LOWER

MUNNS

MILL

DANE LANE

STREET

DANE CLOSE

Sch

Hartlip

HOLLOW LANE

GRAINEY FIELD

P3 SHOUGH CLO

THE

he Index includes some ames for which there is sufficient space on the maps. hese names are indicated by n * and are followed by the earest adjoining thoroughfare.

Abbey Cl ME12 12 D3
Abbey Fields Ct ME13 9 E2
Abbey Flds ME13 9 E3
Abbey Pl ME13 8 D2
Abbey Rd ME13 8 D1
Abbeyview Dr ME12 12 B3
Abbots Rd ME13 9 E2
Acacia Ter ME10 4 D3
Acorn St ME12 14 D3
Addington Rd ME10 5 E3
Adelaide Dr ME10 3 E3
Adelaide Gdns ME12 13 E1
Adisham Grn ME10 3 E3
Admirals Walk ME12 13 F1
Admiralty Cl ME10 3 E3
Albany Rd ME10 5 F3
Albion Pl, Faversham ME13 8 C2
Albion Pl, Sittingbourne ME9 17 E7
Alder Cl ME12 14 B5
Aldred Rd ME13 8 C3
Alexander Cl ME12 8 C2
Alexander Dr ME13 8 B2
Alexandra Cl ME10 3 C4
Alexandra Rd ME12 15 E3
All Saints Rd ME10 6 A3
Allen Ct ME12 12 A4
Allenby Walk ME10 4 C1
Allsworth Cl ME9 17 D7
Alma Rd ME12 14 D3
Alma St ME12 15 E2
Almond Tree Cl ME10 14 B5
Alston Ct ME12 12 C2
Amber Cl ME9 7 B2
Amber Rise ME10 3 B4
Ambleside, Faversham ME13 9 E4
Ambleside, Sittingbourne ME10 6 A4
Anatase Cl ME10 3 B4
Anchor Bsns Pk ME10 5 H1
Anchor La ME12 14 B1
Andrews Walk ME10 4 B2
Anne Boleyn Cl ME12 10 C5
Anselm Cl ME10 5 E3
Appledore Av ME12 14 C5
Appleford Dr ME12 12 A2
Arden Cl ME13 9 E3
Argent Bsns Pk ME11 13 A4
Argent Rd ME11 13 B4
Argent Way ME10 3 B4
Arthur Kennedy Cl ME13 10 B2
Arthur Salmon Cl ME13 8 B3
Arthur St ME10 5 E3
Arundel Av ME10 5 F6
Ashford Rd ME13 8 C5
Ashington Cl ME10 4 D2
Ashley Cl ME12 13 D2
Ashtead Dr ME9 6 B5
Athelstan Rd ME13 8 B3
Athol Pl ME13 8 A2
Attlee Way ME10 5 G3
Aubretia Walk ME10 4 C4
Auckland Dr ME12 12 B1
Augustine Rd ME12 3 E3
Austin Cl ME10 5 E2
Avent Walk ME9 6 C4
Avenue of Remembrance ME10 5 F3
Aylewyn Grn ME10 3 E3

Back La, Faversham ME13 8 D2
Back La, Sheerness ME12 12 D3
Baker Cl ME10 7 B1
Balas Dr ME10 3 A4
Baldwin Rd ME12 12 E3
Balmoral Ter ME10 8 C3
Bank St ME13 13 F1
Banner Way ME10 4 C5
Bannister Hill ME9 5 E3
Barkers Ct ME10 5 E3
Barler Pl ME11 13 B2
Barn Cl ME9 4 B5
Barnes Cl ME13 8 B1
Barnfield Rd ME13 8 C1
Barnsley Cl ME12 15 F2
Barrow Gro ME10 5 E3
Bartletts Cl ME13 13 D2
Barton Hill Dr ME12 12 A4
Bassett Rd ME10 5 E3
Bay View Gdns ME12 11 B3
Bayford Rd ME10 5 H3

Beach App ME12 11 B2
Beach St ME12 14 C2
Beach Ter ME12 14 C2
Beaconsfield Rd ME10 6 A3
Beaumont Davey Cl ME13 8 C4
Beaumont Ter ME13 8 D3
Beauvoir Dr ME10 3 E3
Beckett St ME12 14 C2
Beckley Rd ME12 15 F3
Beech Cl ME13 8 B3
Beechwood Av ME10 5 E1
Belgrave Rd ME12 13 D2
Bell Cotts ME9 16 D2
Bell Rd ME10 5 F5
Belle Friday Cl ME9 7 B2
Bellevue Rd ME12 12 C3
Belmont Rd, Faversham ME13 8 C4
Belmont Rd, Sheerness ME12 15 F6
Belmont Rd, Sittingbourne ME10 5 E4
Belvedere Rd ME10 8 D2
Bensted Gro ME13 8 A3
Berkeley Cl ME10 10 D1
Berkeley Ct ME10 4 D3
Berridge Rd ME10 14 D3
Berry St ME10 5 F3
Bishop La ME9 16 A2
Blacketts Rd ME9 6 D1
Blandford Gdns ME13 5 E6
Blatcher Cl ME12 12 C4
Blaxland Cl ME10 8 B1
Blenheim Av ME13 9 E4
Blenheim Rd ME10 5 H5
Blythe Cl ME10 5 H3
Boat House Rd ME12 14 A1
Bob Amor Cl ME10 9 E3
Bobbing Hill ME9 4 A1
Bonetta Ct ME12 14 C4
Bonham Dr ME10 5 H2
Borden La ME9,10 4 C5
Borough Rd ME11 13 B3
Botany Cl ME10 14 C3
Boughton Hill ME13 10 D2
Boundary Cl ME10 12 E4
Bounds La ME13 10 C2
Bourne Gro ME10 4 D2
Boxley Cl ME12 14 C5
Boxted La ME9 16 C4
Boyces Hill ME9 17 F7
Bracken Cl ME10 6 A2
Bradfield Av ME13 7 B2
Bradley Dr ME10 5 E5
Bradshaw Cl ME9 16 B2
Bramblefield La ME10 3 C2
Bramblehill Rd ME13 8 C2
Bramley Av ME13 9 E4
Bramley Cl, Sheerness ME12 10 C4
Bramley Cl, Sittingbourne ME9 17 D7
Bramley Way ME10 10 C5
Bramston Rd ME12 12 D3
Brasier Ct ME12 12 A4
Breach La ME9 17 B6
Brecon Chase ME12 12 C5
Bredhurst Cl ME12 14 C5
Brenchley Rd ME10 9 H6
Brenley La ME13 8 C2
Brent Hill ME13 8 C2
Brent Rd ME13 8 C2
Brents Ind Est ME13 8 D1
Brewery Rd ME10 5 F1
Briar Rd ME10 4 B2
Brickfield La ME10 10 A2
Brickmakers Bsns Centre ME10 5 H1
Bridge Rd, Faversham ME13 8 D2
Bridge Rd, Sheerness ME12 14 C2
Bridgewater Rd ME12 14 C4
Brielle Way, Queenborough ME11 13 A1
Brielle Way, Sheerness ME12 14 A6
Brisbane Av ME10 4 C3
Britannia Cl ME10 3 D3
Briton Cl ME10 14 C4
Briton Rd ME13 14 C3
Broad St ME12 14 C2
Broadacre ME9 7 C2
Broadway ME12 14 B4
Brogdale Pl ME13 8 B4
Brogdale Rd ME13 8 B5
Brook Rd ME13 8 D1
Brookes Pl ME9 17 E7
Broom Rd ME10 6 A2
Broomfield Rd ME13 8 C1
Bucklers Cl ME12 11 B1
Buddle Dr ME12 15 F5
Bull La, Faversham ME13 10 A1

Bull La, Sittingbourne ME9 17 D8
Burkestone Cl ME10 3 E3
Burley Rd ME10 5 E3
Burham Cl ME10 3 D3
Burnt Oast Rd ME13 10 C2
Burntwick Dr ME9 16 E3
Burnup Bank ME10 6 A2
Bushey Cl ME13 10 A2
Buttermere ME13 9 E4
Bysing Wood Rd ME13 8 A1

Caldew Gro ME10 5 H4
Callaways La ME9 17 E7
Cambridge Rd, Faversham ME13 8 B3
Cambridge Rd, Sittingbourne ME10 5 H4
Camp La ME13 11 D3
Canberra Gdns ME10 4 D3
Canterbury Rd, Boughton Street ME10 10 A1
Canterbury Rd, Faversham ME13 8 D4
Canterbury Rd, Sittingbourne ME10 5 H3
Canute Rd ME13 8 C4
Capel Rd, Faversham ME13 8 B3
Capel Rd, Sittingbourne ME10 5 E4
Cardinal Cl ME12 12 D3
Cardine Cl ME12 3 D4
Carlton Av ME12 14 C4
Castle Rd ME10 5 H3
Castle Rd Bsns Precinct ME10 5 H1
Castle Rd Technical Centre ME10 5 H1
Castle Rough La ME10 3 E2
Castle St ME10 13 A2
Castleacres Ind Est ME10 5 H1
Castlemere Av ME11 13 B2
Cavell Way ME10 4 D2
Cavour Rd, Faversham ME13 8 C3
Cavour Rd, Sheerness ME12 14 D3
Cecil Av ME10 14 C4
Cedar Cl ME10 5 H4
Cellar Hill ME9 7 B3
Celt Cl ME10 3 D3
Central Av ME10 5 F3
Century Rd ME13 9 E3
Ceres Ct ME10 8 B1
Chaffes La ME9 16 A3
Chaffes Ter ME9 16 A3
Chalk Rd ME11 13 A2
Chalkwell Rd ME10 5 E3
Challenger Cl ME10 3 D4
Chapel St, Faversham ME13 8 D3
Chapel St, Minster ME12 12 E3
Chapel St, Sheerness ME12 14 B2
Chappell Way ME10 5 E1
Charles Drayson Ct ME13 9 E2
Charles St ME12 14 B2
Charlotte St ME12 14 B2
Chart Cl ME13 8 B3
Chartwell Gro ME10 3 D4
Chatsworth Dr ME10 4 C2
Chaucer Rd ME10 5 E4
Chegworth Gdns ME10 5 E6
Cheney Rd ME10 9 F3
Chequers Rd ME12 12 F3
Cherry Cl ME10 5 E1
Cherry Gdns ME10 7 B3
Cherry Hill Ct ME9 17 E7
Cherry Tree Cl, Sheerness ME12 14 B5
Cherry Tree Cl, Sittingbourne ME10 7 B2
Cherry Tree Dr ME13 7 A5
Cherryfields ME13 8 B3
Chestnut Cl ME13 10 B2
Chestnut St ME9 4 A2
Cheyne Cl ME13 2 E3
Cheyne Rd ME12 10 C5
Chiddingfold Cl ME12 14 C5
Chilham Cl ME12 14 C5
Chilton Av ME12 5 G3
Church Farm Rd ME9 16 E7
Church Path ME9 16 E2
Church Rd, Bapchild ME9 6 C3
Church Rd, Faversham ME13 8 D2
Church Rd, Oare ME13 7 C5
Church Rd, Sheerness ME12 10 B4
Church Rd, Sittingbourne ME10 5 H3

Church Rd Bsns Centre ME10 6 A1
Church Rd, Bapchild ME9 6 B6
Church St, Faversham ME13 8 D2
Church St, Milton Regis ME10 5 E2
Church St, Sittingbourne ME10 5 E2
Church Ter ME12 12 D3
Churchill Rd ME12 12 E3
Churchill Way ME13 8 B1
Cinnabar Dr ME10 3 A4
Clarence Gdns ME12 11 B2
Clarence Rd ME12 14 D2
Clarence Row ME12 14 D2
Clarendon Cl ME10 5 F6
Clement Cl ME10 3 D3
Clerke Dr ME10 3 E3
Cliff Dr ME12 11 B1
Cliff Gdns ME12 12 E3
Cliff View Gdns, Bay View ME12 11 B4
Cliff View Gdns, Warden ME12 11 C1
Clive Rd ME10 4 C1
Clovelly Dr ME12 12 B2
Clover Ct ME10 5 H2
Cluny Rd ME12 9 E3
Clyde St ME12 15 E3
Coats Av ME12 14 B5
Cobb Walk ME13 8 B2
Cobham Av ME10 5 E6
Cobham Chase ME13 8 B2
Cold Harbour La ME9 4 A1
Coldharbour La ME10 3 E2
Cole Rd ME13 9 E2
Colegates Cl ME13 7 B5
Colegates Ct ME13 7 B5
Colegates Rd ME13 7 A6
Coleman Dr ME10 3 E2
Colfe Way ME10 3 E3
College Rd ME10 4 D5
Collingwood Walk ME10 4 C1
Colonels La ME13 10 B2
Commonwealth Cl ME10 5 H4
Condor Cl ME12 11 C2
Conduit St ME13 8 D2
Connaught Rd ME10 5 E4
Conyer Rd ME9 7 C2
Cooks La ME10 5 F1
Coombe Dr ME10 6 A2
Copland Av ME12 12 C4
Coppins La ME9 4 B5
Coronation Cres ME11 13 A2
Coronation Dr ME12 11 B3
Coronation Rd ME12 15 E3
Cortland Cl ME10 5 H4
Cortland Mws ME10 5 E1
Court Hall ME11 13 A2
Court St ME13 3 D4
Court St ME13 8 D2
Cowper Rd ME10 5 H3
Cranbrook Dr ME10 5 E6
Cremer Pl ME13 8 B2
Cremers Rd ME10 5 H2
Crescent Rd ME13 8 D2
Crescent St ME10 5 F3
Cress Way ME13 8 B3
Cricketers Cl ME10 3 D2
Crispin Cl ME13 8 C1
Cromwell Rd ME10 14 B5
Crosier Ct ME10 16 A2
Cross La, Faversham ME13 8 C3
Cross La, Sittingbourne ME10 5 F1
Crossways ME10 5 F6
Crouch Hill Ct ME9 16 E2
Crown Pk ME10 16 D2
Crown Quay La ME10 5 G3
Crown Rd ME10 5 E1
Cryalls La ME10 4 B3
Cullet St ME12 13 A3
Cumberland Dr ME9 16 E3
Curlew Av ME10 16 D2
Curtis Way ME13 8 C2
Cyprus Rd ME13 9 E3

Daffodil Ho ME9 17 E7
Dalewood ME9 5 H5
Dan Dr ME13 8 A1
Dane Cl ME13 17 A7
Dane La ME9 17 A7
Danedale Av ME12 12 F3
Danes Cl ME12 11 A4
Danes Mead ME10 3 D2
Danley Rd ME12 15 F6
Dark Hill ME13 8 C2
Darlington Dr ME12 12 A4
David Cl ME13 7 B2
Davie Cl ME12 14 C5
Davington Hill ME13 8 C2
Dawes Rd ME10 10 D1
Dean Rd ME10 5 E1

Delamark Rd ME12 14 D2
Denbigh Cl ME10 3 C4
Denham Rd ME9 17 E6
Dennis Willcocks Cl ME9 17 D7
Dental Cl ME10 4 B2
Derby Cl ME10 5 E1
Desmonds Cres ME13 9 G5
Detling Cl ME10 14 C5
Diamond Ct ME10 14 C4
Dickson Ct ME10 5 H3
Diligent Dr ME10 3 D3
Dobbie Ct ME10 3 D4
Does Alley ME10 5 F3
Dolphin Pk ME10 5 H2
Dolphin Rd ME10 5 H2
Donald Moor Av ME9 7 B2
Donemowe Dr ME10 3 E3
Dorset Pl ME13 8 C3
Dorset Rd ME12 14 B4
Dorset Rd Ind Est ME12 14 B4
Doubleday Dr ME9 6 B5
Dover Rd ME12 12 D4
Drake Av ME12 16 A3
Drakes Cl ME13 12 B4
Dreadnought Av ME12 12 B4
Drywall ME10 5 H1
Dully Rd ME9 6 C5
Dumergue Av ME11 13 B3
Dunedin Av ME10 4 D3
Dunkirk Rd North ME13 10 C
Dunkirk Rd South ME13 10 C
Dyngley Cl ME10 3 C

Eadred Way ME10 3 E
Eagles Cl ME10 6 A
East Grn ME10 3 E
East Hall La ME10 6 A
East La ME12 14 B
East St, Faversham ME13 8 D
East St, Sittingbourne ME10 5 G
Eastchurch Rd ME12 10 A
Eastern Av, Halfway Houses ME12 15 E
Eastern Av, Leysdown-on-Sea ME12 11 B
Eastern Av, Queenborough ME11 13 B
Eastling Rd ME13 8 A
Eastwood Rd ME10 5 E
Eaves Ct ME10 12 E
Echo Walk ME12 12 E
Eclipse Dr ME10 3 D
Edenbridge Dr ME12 14 C
Edith Rd ME13 8 C
Edward Rd ME13 13 H
Edwina Av ME12 12 E
Edwins Pl ME9 17 E
Edyngham Cl ME10 3 E
Egbert Rd ME10 8 C
Eleanor Dr ME10 3 E
Ellens Pl ME10 17 E
Elliotts Pl ME13 9 E
Ellison Ct ME13 9 E
Elm Gro ME10 6 E
Elm La ME12 12 E
Emerald Cres ME10 4 E
Emerald Vw ME12 11 E
Empress Gdns ME12 11 E
Ennerdale ME13 9 E
Epps Rd ME10 5 E
Esplanade, Sheerness ME12 14 E
Esplanade, Sheerness ME12 15 E
Esther Ct ME10 15 E
Estuary Rd ME12 14 E
Ethelbert Rd ME13 8 E
Ethelred Ct ME13 8 E
Eurolink Ind Est ME10 5 E
Eurolink Way ME10 5 E
Everard Way ME13 5 E

Fairleas ME10 6 E
Fairservice Cl ME10 6 E
Fairview Rd ME10 6 E
Falcon Ct ME10 12 E
Falcon Gdns ME12 12 E
Fallowfield ME10 6 E
Farm Cres ME10 5 E
Faversham Reach ME13 8 E
Featherbed La ME13 9 E
Feldspar Cl ME10 3 E
Fern Walk ME10 6 E
Ferndale Ct ME10 8 E
Fernleigh Cl ME13 13 E
Fernleigh Ter ME10 8 E
Ferry Vw ME11 13 E
Field End Pl ME13 9 E
Field View Cl ME13 7 E
Fielder Cl ME10 5 E
Fielding St ME13 8 E
Filer ME12 12 E
Finlay Cl ME13 9 E

st Av,
ueenborough ME11 13 A3
st Av,
neerness ME12 14 D3
nders Cl ME10 3 E2
et Av ME12 14 C4
etwood Cl ME12 12 B4
t Cl ME10 3 D3
od La ME13 8 C2
bes Rd ME13 8 C4
ge Cl ME13 8 D4
ge La ME9 16 B2
ge Rd ME10 5 E1
tall Rd ME13 8 C1
untain St ME10 5 F3
Hill ME9 6 B4
xgrove ME10 3 D4
kley Rd ME11 13 A2
nk Apps Cl ME9 17 D7
derick St ME10 5 E3
nches Row ME9 7 C2
nsham Cl ME10 5 H3
bisher Cl ME10 3 D4
gnal Cl ME9 7 A2
gnal Gdns ME9 7 A2
gnal La ME9 7 A2
nt Brents ME13 8 D2
ston Pl ME10 5 G4
ze Hill Cres ME12 13 E1

dby Rd ME10 4 C2
nsborough Cl ME10 4 C2
ena Cl ME10 3 A4
way Rd ME12 14 D3
rison Rd ME12 14 B1
s La ME13 10 A1
s Rd,
ilton Regis ME10 5 F1
s Rd,
ttingbourne ME10 6 A1
efield La ME13 8 D3
hurst Dr ME10 4 C2
e Hill Av ME10 5 H4
nesta Cl ME10 3 D4
orge La ME13 10 B1
orge St ME10 5 H3
orgian Cl ME11 13 B4
rards Dr ME10 5 F5
bons Rd ME10 4 C2
son St ME10 5 E3
aud Dr ME13 8 B1
dstone Dr ME10 6 A3
be La ME10 5 H5
nbrook Gro ME10 3 C4
ndale Rd ME12 12 C2
nwood Dr ME12 12 C3
ver Cl ME10 3 E2
vers Cres ME10 5 F4
dwin Cl ME10 3 D2
dfinch Cl ME13 8 C1
odnestone Rd ME10 5 H3
don Av ME11 13 B2
don Cl ME10 6 B3
don Rd ME13 9 E2
rdon Sq ME13 9 E2
e Cotts ME9 16 B4
e Court Rd ME10 5 E5
rse Rd ME10 6 A2
ce Rd ME12 14 B3
fton Rd ME10 5 F3
fton Way ME10 5 G3
iney Fld ME9 17 A8
nville Cl ME13 8 C2
nville Pl ME12 14 D3
nville Rd ME12 14 C3
veney Rd ME13 9 F3
yling Ct ME10 4 D4
yshott Cl ME10 5 G4
at Basin Rd ME12 14 B2
en Porch Cl ME10 3 E4
enlees Cl ME10 4 B2
enway ME13 8 B2
enways,
wer Halstow ME9 16 D2
enways,
ttingbourne ME10 5 H4
egory Cl ME10 3 E3
ve Av ME12 11 E3
ve Cl ME13 8 A3
ve Park Av ME10 4 B2
ve Pl ME13 8 A3
vehurst Av ME10 3 D3
vehurst Rd ME9 3 D1

es Rd ME10 4 D6
way Rd ME12 15 E4
Cl ME10 5 F1
stow La ME9 16 C2
n Rd ME13 8 C1
nbrook Walk ME10 3 D3
hilton Cres ME10 4 C3
over Cl ME10 5 F4
kness Ct ME10 5 H3
old Ct ME13 8 C4
old Rd ME10 5 H3
old St ME11 13 B3
os Av ME12 12 C3
ier Dr ME10 5 G4
is Gdns ME10 6 A2
is Rd ME12 14 D3
ison Ter ME13 7 B5

Harrys Rd ME9 7 B1
Hartlip Cl ME12 14 C6
Harvey Dr ME10 5 G5
Hasted Rd ME9 17 E6
Hatch St ME13 8 C2
Hawkins Cl ME10 3 D4
Hawthorn Av ME12 14 B5
Hawthorn Rd ME10 5 E2
Haysel ME10 5 G5
Hazebrouck Rd ME13 8 A2
Hazel Gro ME12 15 H4
Heard Way ME10 5 H2
Hearne Cl ME10 6 A2
Hearts Delight ME9 4 B6
Hearts Delight Rd ME9 4 B6
Heather Cl ME10 5 G3
Hempstead La ME9 6 C4
Heron Cl ME9 16 E2
Heron Dr ME12 12 C4
Hever Pl ME10 4 D4
High St, Blue Town ME12 14 D2
High St,
Eastchurch ME12 10 B4
High St,
Milton Regis ME10 5 F1
High St, Minster ME12 12 D3
High St, Newington ME9 17 E7
High St,
Queenborough ME11 13 A2
High St,
Sheerness ME12 14 B2
High St,
Sittingbourne ME10 5 F3
Highfield Rd ME12 13 F1
Highsted Rd ME10 5 F4
Highview Cl ME13 10 C2
Highview Rd ME12 12 D3
Hilda Rd ME12 13 E1
Hill Brow ME10 4 D4
Hillside Av ME11 13 A4
Hillside Rd ME12 12 B2
Hilltop Rd ME12 12 A4
Hilton Cl ME13 8 D4
Hilton Dr ME10 4 C1
Hinde Cl ME10 3 E4
Hobart Gdns ME10 4 D3
Holland Cl ME12 14 C3
Hollow La ME9 17 A8
Holmside Av ME12 13 E1
Holyrood Dr ME12 12 A4
Holywell La ME9 16 C2
Home Vw ME10 5 H3
Homestall La ME13 9 H3
Homestead Vw ME9 4 B5
Homewood Av ME10 4 D3
Honeyball Walk ME9 7 B2
Honeysuckle Ct ME10 5 H2
Hope St,
Sheerness ME12 14 D2
Hope St,
Sheerness ME12 14 C3
Hopsons Pl ME12 12 D4
Horselees Rd ME13 10 C3
Horsford Walk ME13 8 B1
Horsham Hill ME9 16 A2
Horsham La ME9 16 A2
Howard Av ME10 5 E1
Howard Cl ME12 12 D2
Hugh Pl ME13 8 D2
Hugh Price Cl ME10 6 A1
Hurst La ME10 3 D2
Hutchings Cl ME10 6 A2
Hythe Rd ME10 5 E1

Imperial Av ME12 12 D3
Imperial Dr ME12 11 B1
Ingleden Cl ME10 3 E3
Institute Rd ME13 8 D3
Invicta Ct ME10 3 D3
Invicta Rd ME12 14 D3
Ivory Cl ME13 8 A1

Jacinth Dr ME10 4 D1
Jade Cl ME10 3 B4
James St ME12 15 E3
Jefferson Rd ME12 15 E3
Jessica Mws ME10 3 C4
Jetty Rd,
Sheerness ME12 14 A2
Jetty Rd, Warden ME12 11 C1
John Hall Cl ME13 7 C6
Johnson Ct ME13 8 B1
Johnson Rd ME10 5 E3
Johnson Way ME12 12 B3
Jubilee Cres ME11 13 A2
Jubilee St ME10 5 E2
Judd Rd ME13 8 A3

Kenilworth Ct ME10 4 C2
Kennedy Cl ME13 8 D1
Kent Av,
Sheerness ME12 12 B2
Kent Av,
Sittingbourne ME10 4 D4
Kent Rd ME12 14 C3
Kent St ME12 14 B2
Kent View Dr ME12 10 B6
Kestrel Cl ME10 5 G4
Keswick Av ME10 6 A3
Key St ME10 4 B2
Keycol Hill ME9 4 A2

Kiln Cl ME10 5 G4
Kiln Ct ME13 8 A2
King St,
Sheerness ME12 14 B2
King St,
Sittingbourne ME10 5 F1
Kings Head Alley ME12 14 B2
Kings Mill Cl ME10 5 E1
Kings Rd,
Faversham ME13 8 C3
Kings Rd,
Sheerness ME12 12 D3
Kingsnorth Rd ME13 8 C4
Klondyke Ind Est ME11 13 A3
Knightsfield Rd ME10 3 B4
Knoll Way ME12 11 B1

Laburnum Pl ME10 5 E2
Labworth Cl ME12 13 E1
Lammas Dr ME10 5 E1
Lammas Gate ME13 8 D1
Lance Cl ME10 3 D3
Landrail Rd ME9 16 D3
Langley Rd ME10 3 D4
Lansdown Rd ME10 6 A3
Lapwing Cl ME12 12 C4
Lapwing Dr ME9 16 E2
Larch Ter ME12 14 B5
Larkfield Av ME10 5 E1
Larksfield Rd ME13 8 C1
Lavender Ct ME10 5 G4
Laxton Way,
Faversham ME13 9 E4
Laxton Way,
Sittingbourne ME10 5 E1
Leach Ho ME13 10 C2
Leicester Gdns ME12 11 B2
Leigh Ct ME12 12 A4
Les Spickett Cl ME13 9 E4
Leslie Smith Dr ME13 8 C2
Lewis Cl ME13 8 A2
Leysdown Rd,
Eastchurch ME12 10 C4
Leysdown Rd,
Leysdown-on-Sea ME12 11 A4
Liege Cl ME10 3 D2
Lime Gro,
Sheerness ME12 13 D2
Lime Gro,
Sittingbourne ME10 5 G3
Linden Cl ME10 5 E4
Linden Dr ME12 14 B5
Lindfield Cotts ME13 8 A3
Lion Fld ME13 8 A3
Lion Yd ME13 8 A3
Little Glovers ME10 5 F4
Lomas Rd ME10 6 A3
London Rd, Bapchild ME9 6 C4
London Rd,
Faversham ME13 8 B4
London Rd,
Newington ME9 17 A6
London Rd,
Sittingbourne ME10 4 B2
London Rd, Teynham ME9 7 A2
London Rd Trading Est ME10 5 E3
Longridge ME10 5 H5
Lonsdale Dr ME10 4 C2
Lords Cl ME9 6 C5
Lorimar Ct ME10 3 B4
Love La,
Faversham ME13 9 E5
Love La,
Sheerness ME12 12 D2
Lovell Rd ME12 12 A4
Lower Hartlip Rd ME9 17 A8
Lower Rd, Bapchild ME9 6 D3
Lower Rd,
Eastchurch ME12 10 A4
Lower Rd,
Faversham ME13 8 A3
Lower Rd, Minster ME12 13 E3
Lower Rd, Teynham ME9 7 B1
Lower Rd, Teynham ME9 7 C2
Lowfield Rd ME12 13 F1
Luton Rd ME13 9 E3
Lydbrook Cl ME10 4 D3
Lyndhurst Gro ME10 5 E5
Lynmouth Dr ME12 12 D2
Lynsted La ME9 7 A3
Lynsted Rd ME12 15 F6

Macknade Farm Cotts ME13 9 E5
Magpie Ct ME12 12 B3
Main Rd,
Queenborough ME11 13 B2
Main Rd,
Sheerness ME12 14 B2
Maitland Ct ME13 8 B1
Makenade Av ME13 8 D4
Mallard Ct ME12 12 B3
Manor Cl ME11 13 A4
Manor Gro ME10 5 E4
Manor Rd ME11 13 A4
Manor Way ME12 11 E3
Manwood Cl ME10 5 F5
Maple St ME12 14 D4
Marian Av ME12 12 A3

Marina Dr ME12 12 B3
Marine Par ME12 15 E2
Market Pl ME13 8 D2
Market St ME13 8 D3
Marr Cl ME12 12 A3
Marsh Rise ME10 3 F2
Marshall Cres ME11 13 A4
Marstan Cl ME9 16 A3
Maylam Gdns ME10 4 B3
Medway Cl ME10 5 E3
Medway Rd ME12 14 C3
Meeres Court La ME10 6 A1
Mellor Row ME10 3 E2
Melody Cl ME12 11 B1
Mendfield St ME13 8 C2
Menin Rd ME10 3 E2
Menzies Ct ME12 12 A4
Merleburgh Dr ME10 3 E3
Merlin Cl ME10 5 G4
Meteor Cl ME10 3 D3
Meyrick Rd ME12 14 D2
Micketts Gdns ME10 4 B3
Middle Row ME13 8 D2
Middletune Av ME10 3 C4
Middleway ME10 5 H4
Milbourne Gro ME10 3 C4
Mile Town Ind Est ME12 14 B3
Mill Ct ME10 5 G4
Mill Hill ME12 12 E3
Mill La ME9 17 A7
Mill Way ME10 5 F1
Millen Rd ME10 5 E2
Millennium Way ME12 14 C2
Miller Cl ME10 3 F3
Miller Ct ME12 12 A4
Millfield ME10 5 G4
Millfield Rd ME13 9 E3
Mills Cl ME12 12 A3
Millstream Cl ME13 8 C2
Milsted Cl ME12 14 C5
Milton Rd ME10 5 F2
Minster Dr ME12 12 C2
Minster Rd,
Faversham ME13 9 E3
Minster Rd,
Sheerness ME12 13 F1
Minterne Av ME10 4 D5
Miranda Ct ME12 14 C4
Moat Way ME11 13 B2
Monks Cl ME13 8 B2
Mons Ct ME10 3 E2
Montague Ct ME12 14 C4
Moonfleet Cl ME10 3 E2
Morello Cl ME9 7 B2
Morris Court Cl ME9 6 B5
Mortuary Rd ME12 14 B2
Mount Fld,
Faversham ME13 8 B3
Mount Fld,
Queenborough ME11 13 B2
Mount Pleasant ME13 7 B5
Mountview ME9 4 B5
Munns La ME9 17 A7
Murston Rd ME10 5 H3
Murthwaite Ct ME12 12 A4
Musgrave Rd ME10 5 F1
Mustards Rd ME12 11 A3
Mutton La ME13 8 A4

Napier Cl ME10 4 D3
Napleton Rd ME13 8 C2
Nativity Cl ME10 5 E3
Nautilus Cl ME12 12 B4
Nautilus Dr ME12 12 B4
Neats Ct ME11 13 B4
Nelson Av ME12 12 D4
Nelson Cl ME12 14 B4
Nelson Gdns ME13 8 C4
Nelson St ME13 8 C4
Nelson Ter ME13 8 C4
Nelson Walk ME10 4 C1
Neptune Ter ME12 15 E2
New Gardens Rd ME9 7 B2
New La ME12 14 D3
New Rd, Minster ME12 12 C4
New Rd,
Sheerness ME12 14 B5
New Rd Ind Est ME12 14 B3
New St ME12 14 C3
Newbridge Av ME10 3 D4
Newcomen Rd ME12 14 D2
Newington Enterprise Centre ME9 17 E5
Newington Ind Est ME9 17 C7
Newland Rd ME12 14 B5
Newlands Av ME10 4 C2
Newman Dr ME10 3 E3
Newton Rd ME13 8 D3
Nightingale Rd ME13 8 C3
Nobel Cl ME9 7 B2
Nobel Ct ME13 8 B3
Nore Cl ME12 14 D3
Noreen Av ME12 12 A3
Norman Rd ME13 8 C3
Normans Wood Ct ME12 15 E3
North La,
Boughton-under-Blean ME13 10 B3

North La,
Faversham ME13 8 C2
North Rd ME11 13 A2
North St ME10 3 D4
Northwood Dr ME10 5 F6
Norwood Rise ME12 12 C2
Norwood Walk ME10 4 C1
Norwood Walk West ME10 4 C1
Nouds La ME9 7 C3
Nursery Cl ME12 15 E3
Nutberry Cl ME9 7 C2
Nutfields ME10 5 H4
Nutts Av ME12 11 E3

Oak Av ME12 12 F3
Oak Dr ME13 10 C2
Oak La, Sheerness ME12 12 F3
Oak La,
Sittingbourne ME9 16 A4
Oak Rd ME10 6 A3
Oakfields ME10 4 D3
Oare Rd ME13 7 C6
Oast Ct ME10 5 F5
Ocean Ter,
Bay View ME12 11 B3
Ocean Ter, Minster ME12 12 E3
Old Gate Rd ME13 8 B2
Old House La ME9 17 A8
Olivine Cl ME10 3 B4
Orchard Dr ME9 17 D8
Orchard Gro ME12 12 C3
Orchard Pl,
Faversham ME13 8 D3
Orchard Pl,
Sittingbourne ME10 5 G4
Orchard Vw ME9 7 B2
Orchard Way ME12 10 B6
Osborne Ct ME13 8 A2
Osier Rd ME9 7 C1
Osprey Ct ME10 5 G4
Ospringe Pl ME13 8 B4
Ospringe Rd ME13 8 B3
Ospringe St ME13 8 A3
Ostend Ct ME10 3 E2
Outnalls ME12 14 D3
Oyster Cl ME10 5 F1

Paddock Rd ME12 14 B2
Palmerston Walk ME10 6 A3
Panteny La ME9 6 B5
Paradise Gdns ME12 11 D4
Parish Cl ME12 12 B4
Parish Rd ME12 12 B4
Park Av,
Queenborough ME11 13 B3
Park Av, Sheerness ME12 11 E4
Park Av,
Sittingbourne ME10 5 E5
Park Dr ME10 5 E6
Park Rd,
Faversham ME13 8 D3
Park Rd,
Queenborough ME11 13 A2
Park Rd,
Sheerness ME12 15 E4
Park Rd,
Sittingbourne ME10 5 E4
Parsonage Chase ME12 12 A4
Parsonage La ME9 3 A4
Partridge La ME13 8 D2
Pastime Cl ME10 3 D3
Pavilion Dr ME10 3 D2
Pear Tree Walk ME9 17 D7/8
Peel Dr ME10 6 A3
Pembury St ME10 5 F3
Penn Cl ME10 5 H5
Penshurst Rise ME13 8 B2
Pepys Av ME12 14 C2
Peregrine Dr ME10 5 G4
Periwinkle Cl ME10 5 E2
Perth Gdns ME10 4 D3
Petfield Cl ME12 12 D3
Pettits Row ME13 8 B3
Phillippa Ct ME10 3 D3
Pier Rd ME11 14 A6
Pippin Cl ME10 3 C4
Plantation Rd ME13 8 C3
Playstool Cl ME9 17 D7
Playstool Rd ME9 17 D7
Pleasant Pl ME12 13 F1
Plover Rd ME12 12 B4
Pond Dr ME10 5 G4
Pond Farm Rd ME9 4 A6
Poot La ME9 16 B1
Porter Cl ME12 12 B3
Portland Av ME10 6 A2
Poulsen Ct ME10 5 H3
Power Station Rd ME12 15 F5
Prentis Cl ME10 4 C2
Preston Av ME13 9 E4
Preston Gro ME13 8 D4
Preston Hall Gdns ME12 11 B1
Preston La ME13 8 D4
Preston Pk ME13 8 D4
Preston St ME13 8 D3
Primrose Ct ME9 17 E6
Prince Charles Av,
Sheerness ME12 12 D4
Prince Charles Av,
Sittingbourne ME10 6 A4

Princes Av ME12	12 D3	St Peters Rd ME13	10 C2	Stanley Av,		Waterside Vw ME12	11 B
Priory Ct ME12	11 E4	St Saviours Cl ME13	9 E3	Sheerness ME12	12 E3	The Street,	Watling Pl ME10	5 G
Priory Pl ME13	8 C1	St Stephens Cl ME9	17 E6	Staple Cl ME10	5 E1	Lower Halstow ME9	16 D2	Watsons Hill ME10	5 E
Priory Rd ME13	8 C2	Salisbury Cl ME10	6 A3	Staplehurst Rd ME10	4 C1	The Street, Oare ME13	7 C5	Waverley Av ME12	12 B
Priory Row ME13	8 C1	Salmon Cres ME12	12 A3	Staplestreet Rd ME13	10 C1	The Street,		Weald Ct ME10	5 E
Puttney St ME10	3 E3	Salters La ME13	8 D6	Station Pl ME12	5 F3	Upchurch ME9	16 B2	Well Rd ME11	13 A
		Sand Ct ME12	11 D3	Station Rd,		The Tracies ME9	17 E7	Wellesley Rd ME12	15 E
Quay La ME13	8 D2	Sanders Ct ME12	12 A4	Faversham ME13	8 D3	The Wall ME10	5 F2	Wellington Rd ME12	5 F
Queenborough Bsns Centre		Sandford Rd ME10	4 B2	Station Rd,		The Willows,		Wells Rd ME10	6 A
ME11	**13 A4**	Sandstone Dr ME10	3 D2	Newington ME9	17 E7	Kemsley ME10	3 E2	Wells Way ME13	8 E
Queenborough Dr ME12	12 B3	Sanspareil Av ME12	12 A4	Station Rd, Teynham ME9	17 D7	The Willows,		Wellwinch Rd ME10	4 C
Queenborough Rd ME12	13 C2	Satis Av ME10	3 D4	Station Row ME13	7 C1	Newington ME9	17 D7	Wentworth Dr ME10	4 E
Queens Rd,		Saxon Av ME10	12 B3	Station St ME10	5 F3	The Willows,		West Grn ME10	3 E
Faversham ME13	8 B3	Saxon Rd ME13	8 C3	Step Style ME10	5 H5	Sheerness ME12	15 H4	West La, East St,	
Queens Rd,		Saxon Shore ME10	3 F2	Stephens Cl ME13	8 B2	Thistle Hill Way ME12	12 C4	Sittingbourne ME10	5 G
Sheerness ME12	12 D3	Scarborough Dr ME12	12 B1	Sterling Rd,		Thistle Walk ME10	6 A2	West La, West La Trading Est,	
Queens Way ME12	14 B5	School La, Bapchild ME9	6 C3	Queenborough ME11	13 B2	Thomas Rd,		Sittingbourne ME10	5 H
Quickstep Cl ME10	3 D3	School La, Borden ME9	4 A3	Sterling Rd,		Faversham ME13	8 C2	**West La Trading Est**	
Quinton Rd ME10	5 E2	School Rd,		Sittingbourne ME10	4 D6	Thomas Rd,		**ME10**	**5 G**
		Faversham ME13	10 B1	Stickfast Le ME10	3 A2	Sittingbourne ME10	5 H3	West Ridge ME10	5 E
Railway Rd ME12	14 C3	School La,		Stiles Cl ME13	12 A3	Thorn Hill Rd ME12	11 B1	West St, Faversham ME13	8 C
Railway Ter ME11	13 A2	Lower Halstow ME9	16 E3	Stockers Hill ME13	10 A1	Thorn Walk ME10	6 A2	West St,	
Raleigh Way ME12	13 F1	School La,		Stone St ME10	8 C3	Thread Le ME10	4 D1	Sheerness ME12	14 E
Randle Way ME9	6 C5	Newington ME9	17 D5	Stonebridge Way ME13	8 B3	Todd Cres ME10	3 F3	West St,	
Ranelagh Rd ME12	14 D2	School Rd,		Stonedane St ME13	8 C1	Tonge Rd ME10	4 C1	Sittingbourne ME10	5
Recreation Way ME10	3 E2	Faversham ME13	8 B3	Stoney Rd ME10	10 D1	Topaz Dr ME10	4 D1	Westbourne St ME10	5
Rectory Rd ME10	5 H5	School Rd,		Strode Cres ME12	14 D2	Tourmaline Dr ME10	4 D1	Westcliff Dr ME12	12
Red Robin Cotts ME9	17 E7	Sittingbourne ME10	5 H4	Summerville Av ME10	12 C4	Tribune Ct ME10	14 C4	Westerham Rd ME10	4
Reedland Cres ME13	8 C1	Scocles Rd ME12	12 C4	Summerville Cl*,		Tribune Dr ME10	3 D4	Western Av ME12	12
Regency Cl ME10	5 E2	Scoones Cl ME10	6 C5	Gordon Sq ME13	9 E2	Triggs Row ME9	7 C2	Western Link ME13	8
Regis Cres ME10	3 D4	Scotchmen Cl ME13	15 F5	Sumpter Way ME10	8 A2	Trinity Pl ME12	14 D2	Westfield Cotts ME9	16
Rettendon Dr ME10	3 D3	Scraps Hill ME9	12 A3	Sunny Bank ME10	5 H2	Trinity Rd,		Westgate Rd ME13	9
Rhode Ct ME10	4 D2	Scrapsgate ME12	11 B1	Sunnyfields Dr ME12	13 D1	Sheerness ME12	14 D2	Westlands Av ME10	5
Richmond Dr ME10	3 D3	Sea App ME12	11 B2	Sunnyside Cl ME12	12 A3	Trinity Rd,		Westmoreland Dr ME9	16
Richmond St ME12	15 E3	Sea View Gdns ME12	11 B2	Sunstone Dr ME10	4 D1	Sittingbourne ME10	3 E4	Westwood Pl ME13	8
Riddles Rd ME10	4 C4	Seager Rd,		Susans La ME9	16 C2	**Trinity Trading Est**		Westwood Walk ME9	17
Ridham Av ME10	3 E2	Faversham ME13	7 C6	Swale Av,		**ME10**	**3 E4**	Wharf Way ME10	5
River Vw ME11	13 A4	Seager Rd,		Queenborough ME11	13 A4	Trotts Hall Gdns ME10	5 F4	Wheatcroft Cl ME10	5
Riverhead Cl ME10	4 D4	Sheerness ME12	15 F2	Swale Av,		Tunstall Rd ME10	5 E6	Wheatsheaf Cl ME13	10
Rivers Rd ME9	7 C2	Seasalter Cl ME12	11 C1	Sheerness ME12	14 C3	Turmine Ct ME10	12 A4	Wheatsheaf Gdns ME12	14
Roberts Cl ME10	3 C4	Seaside Av ME12	12 C2	Swan Cl ME10	5 H3	Turner Ct ME10	3 E3	Whimbrel Cl ME10	3
Rock Rd ME10	5 E3	Seathorpe Av ME12	12 D2	Swanstree Av ME10	5 H5	Turners Cl ME12	14 D3	Whitehall Rd ME10	5
Rodmer Cl ME10	12 C2	Seaview Av ME12	11 F4	Sydney Av ME10	4 D3	Tysoe Ct ME12	12 A4	Whiteway Rd ME11	13
Roebuck Rd ME13	8 A3	Second Av,		Symmonds Dr ME12	5 G1			Whiting Cres ME13	8
Rolls Av ME10	10 B6	Queenborough ME11	13 A4			**U**fton Le ME10	5 E4	Whitstable Rd,	
Rolvenden Dr ME10	4 C2	Second Av,		**T**aillour St ME10	3 E3	Union Rd ME12	12 D3	Faversham ME13	8
Roman Rd ME13	8 C3	Sheerness ME12	14 C4	Tams Gdns ME12	12 E3	Union St,		Whitstable Rd,	
Roman Sq ME10	5 F3	Selling Rd ME13	9 E5	Tanners St ME13	8 C3	Faversham ME13	8 D3	Faversham ME13	8
Romney Ct ME10	5 E1	Selwood Cl ME12	13 E1	Tavistock Cl ME10	4 D3	Union St,		Whybornes Chase ME12	12
Rook La ME9	4 A1	Sevenacre Rd ME13	8 C1	Telescope Alley ME13	15 E3	Sheerness ME12	14 B2	Wickham Cl ME9	17
Roonagh Ct ME10	5 F5	Sexburga Dr ME12	12 B1	Temple Gdns ME10	5 H4	Unity St,		Wihtred Rd ME9	6
Roper Rd ME9	7 B1	Shakespeare Rd ME12	5 H3	Tenby Ct ME13	8 C3	Sheerness ME12	15 E3	Wildish Rd ME13	8
Rose St ME10	17 D6	Shearwater Ct ME12	14 C4	Terrace Rd ME10	5 H3	Unity St,		Willement Rd ME13	8
Rose St ME12	14 C3	**Sheerness Harbour Est**		Thames Av ME10	5 H4	Sittingbourne ME10	5 E4	William Rigby Dr ME12	15
Rosebery Cl ME10	6 B3	**ME12**	**14 A3**	Thames Ct ME10	11 D3	Uplands Way ME12	13 C2	William St,	
Roseleigh Rd ME10	4 D6	Sheerness Rd ME9	16 E2	The Broadway ME10	12 B1	Uplees Rd ME13	7 A4	Faversham ME13	8
Rosemary Av ME12	13 D1	Sheerways ME10	8 A3	The Burrs ME10	5 G4	Upper Brents ME13	8 D2	William St,	
Roundel Cl ME9	7 C2	Sheet Glass Rd ME11	13 A4	The Butts ME10	5 F3	Upper Field Rd ME10	5 H2	Sittingbourne ME10	5
Rowetts Way ME12	10 B4	Shellness Rd ME10	11 E4	The Charltons ME13	10 B1	Upper St Ann Rd ME13	8 B4	Willis Ct ME12	5
Royal Rd ME12	14 D2	Sheppey St ME13	14 B2	The Cloisters ME10	8 C4			Willow Av ME13	8
Ruby Cl ME10	3 B4	Sheppey Way,		The Close ME13	8 C4	**V**aliennes Rd ME10	5 F3	Wilton Ter ME10	5
Rule Ct ME12	14 C4	Sheerness ME12	13 E4	The Crescent,		Van Rd ME10	5 F3	Windermere ME13	8
Runnymede Mws ME12	8 C3	Sheppey Way,		Faversham ME13	10 C2	Vaughan Dr ME10	3 E3	Windermere Gro ME10	4
Rushenden Cl ME11	13 A4	Sittingbourne ME10	4 A2	The Crescent,		Vectis Dr ME10	3 D3	Windmill Rd ME10	4
Rushenden Rd ME11	13 A4	Sherwood Dr ME13	8 B1	Kemsley ME10	3 E2	Vicarage Ct ME9	17 E6	Windmill Rise ME12	12
Russell Cl ME10	4 C4	Short St ME12	14 C2	The Crescent,		Vicarage La,		Windsor Dr ME10	4
Russell Pl ME13	7 B5	Shortlands Rd ME10	5 H3	Sheerness ME12	13 E1	Faversham ME13	8 A4	Windsor Gdns ME12	11
Russell St ME12	5 H2	Shrubsole Av ME12	14 D3	The Crescent,		Vicarage La,		Wing Rd ME10	12
Russet Av ME13	9 E4	Shurland Av,		Teynham ME9	7 C1	Sittingbourne ME9	16 E2	Winstanley Rd ME12	14
		Leysdown-on-Sea ME12	11 E4	The Fairway ME10	5 F6	Vicarage Rd,		Wises La ME9	14
Saffron Way ME10	3 E4	Shurland Av,		The Fieldings ME10	5 F5	Sheerness ME12	12 D3	Wood St ME12	14
St Agnes Gdns ME12	14 D4	Minster ME12	12 B3	The Finches ME10	5 G4	Vicarage Rd,		Woodberry Dr ME10	5
St Anns Rd ME13	8 B3	Shurland Av,		The Forum ME10	5 F3	Sittingbourne ME10	3 C4	Woodcourt Cl ME10	5
St Catherines Dr ME13	8 D4	Sittingbourne ME10	5 F6	The Glen ME12	12 B,C2	Victoria Pl ME13	8 D2	Woodgate Cl ME13	9
St Clements Cl ME13	11 B3	Silver Birches ME12	15 H4	The Green,		Victoria Rd ME10	14 D4	Woodland Dr ME12	12
St Clements Rd ME12	11 B2	Silverdale Av ME12	12 A3	Sheerness ME12	15 H4	Victoria St ME12	14 C2	Woodlands Rd ME10	4
St Georges Av,		Silverdale Gro ME10	4 C2	The Green,		Victory St ME12	14 C2	Woodside ME13	10
Eastchurch ME12	10 B6	Simpson Rd ME10	5 G4	Sittingbourne ME9	16 D2	Vincent Ct ME12	14 D4	Woodside Gdns ME10	5
St Georges Cl ME10	14 C5	**Sittingbourne Ind Pk**		The Knole ME13	8 B2	Vincent Gdns ME12	14 D4	Woodstock Rd ME10	4
St Georges Ct ME10	14 C4	**ME10**	**5 F2**	The Larches ME13	8 A2	Vincent Rd ME10	6 A3	Woollett Rd ME10	4
St Helens Rd ME12	15 E3	Slipway Rd ME12	14 B1	The Leas ME13	8 B2	Viners Cl ME10	5 F5	Worcester Cl,	
St James Cl ME12	11 B1	Smack Alley ME10	8 D2	The Mall ME13	8 C4	Volante Dr ME10	3 C4	Faversham ME13	9
St Johns Av ME10	5 H4	Smeed Ct ME10	5 H3	The Maltings ME10	8 D1			Worcester Cl,	
St Johns Rd ME13	8 D3	Solomans La ME13	8 D3	The Maples ME12	12 B3	**W**adham Pl ME10	5 H5	Sheerness ME12	15
St Katherine Rd ME12	15 F5	Somerset Cl ME10	4 C3	The Meadows ME10	5 F5	Wallbridge La ME9	16 A3	Worcester Dr ME10	5
St Laurence Cl ME9	6 B5	Sonora Way ME10	1 C1	The Meads Av ME10	3 B4	Wallers Rd ME13	8 A3	Wreight Cl ME13	8
St Marks Cl ME9	17 E6	South Rd ME10	5 G4	The Mews ME10	5 F4	Walmer Gdns ME10	5 E2	Wykeham Cl ME11	1
St Martins Cl ME9	17 E6	South St ME10	13 A2	The Poles ME10	16 B1	Walnut Tree Dr ME10	5 F3	Wykeham Rd ME10	5
St Marys Pl ME9	17 E6	South St ME11	13 A2	The Promenade ME12	11 E3	Walsby Dr ME10	11 C2	Wyllie Ct ME10	4
St Marys Rd ME13	8 D3	Southdown Rd ME10	13 E1	The Ridgeway ME10	10 C2	Warden Bay Rd ME12	10 B4	Wyvern Cl ME10	3
St Marys Row ME12	12 A3	Southsea Av ME12	12 B1	The Rise,		Warden Dr ME12	10 B4		
St Marys Vw ME9	17 E6	Southview Gdns ME12	14 D4	Sheerness ME12	15 H4	Warden View Gdns ME12	11 A4	**Y**eates Dr ME10	4
St Matthews Cl ME9	17 E6	Spillett Cl ME10	8 C3	The Rise,		Wards Hill Rd ME12	12 B1	Yevele Cl ME11	1
St Michaels Cl ME10	5 G3	Springfield Rd ME10	8 C1	Sittingbourne ME9	4 C5	Wardwell La ME9	17 E6	Ypres Dr ME10	5
St Michaels Rd ME10	5 F3	Springhead Rd ME13	8 C1	The Roundel ME10	5 F5	Warren Cl ME10	6 A5		
St Nicholas Rd ME13	8 A3	Sprotshill Cl ME10	3 D4	The Rowans ME12	12 B3	Warwick Cres ME10	4 C2		
St Pauls Av ME13	8 A3	Squires Ct ME10	10 C4	The Square ME10	3 E2	Water La,			
St Pauls Cres ME13	10 C2	Stable Ct ME13	8 D3	The Street, Bapchild ME9	6 B4	Faversham ME13	8 D2		
St Pauls Rd ME13	10 C2	Stadium Way ME10	6 A1	The Street, Borden ME9	4 B4	Water La,			
St Pauls St ME10	5 E2	Stamford Villas ME12	10 B6	The Street,		Ospringe ME13	8 A6		
St Peters Cl ME12	13 D1	Stanhope Av ME10	5 G4	Boughton Street ME13	10 B2	Waterloo Hill ME10	12 D3		
St Peters Ct ME13	8 A3	Stanley Av,		The Street, Hartlip ME9	17 A8	Waterloo Rd ME10	4 D2		
		Queenborough ME11	13 B3			Waterside ME13	8 D1		